CU00652438

Cornwall

BRADWELL
BOOKS

A TASTE OF THE CORNISH COASTLINE

ST. AGNES · KYNANCE COVE · PERRANPORTH · BEDRUTHAN STEPS · GLORIOUS THRIFT

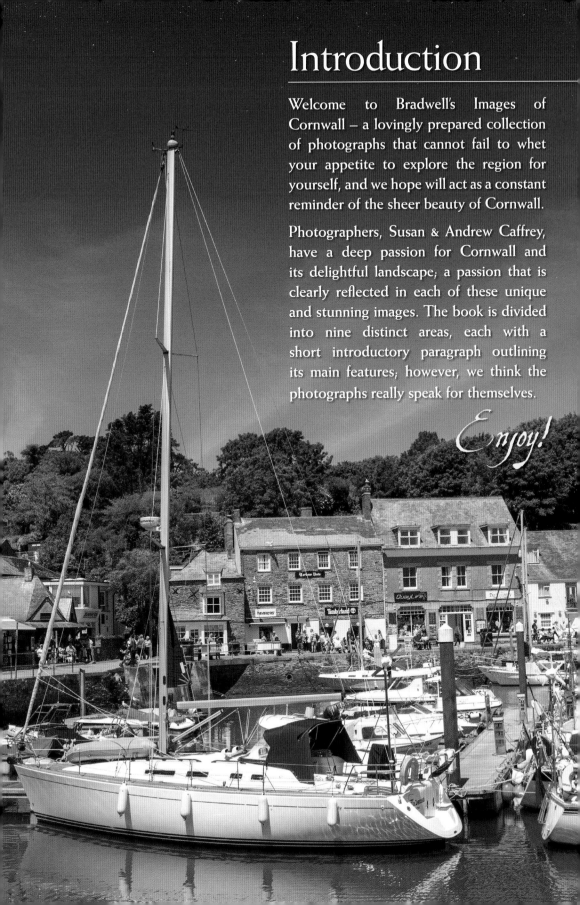

Introduction

Welcome to Bradwell's Images of Cornwall – a lovingly prepared collection of photographs that cannot fail to whet your appetite to explore the region for yourself, and we hope will act as a constant reminder of the sheer beauty of Cornwall.

Photographers, Susan & Andrew Caffrey, have a deep passion for Cornwall and its delightful landscape, a passion that is clearly reflected in each of these unique and stunning images. The book is divided into nine distinct areas, each with a short introductory paragraph outlining its main features; however, we think the photographs really speak for themselves.

Enjoy!

Land's End
Penn an wlas

Marking the most south-westerly point of mainland Britain, Land's End is considered one of the country's most magnificent natural sites. With sweeping views across the Atlantic Ocean and a stunning array of wildlife, a stroll along the iconic Cornish coastline is the perfect way to start exploring the region.

The Land's End complex

Evening on the Land's End coastal path

Enys Dodnan rock formation with Longships lighthouse in the distance

Lichen covered rocks with Land's End complex in the distance

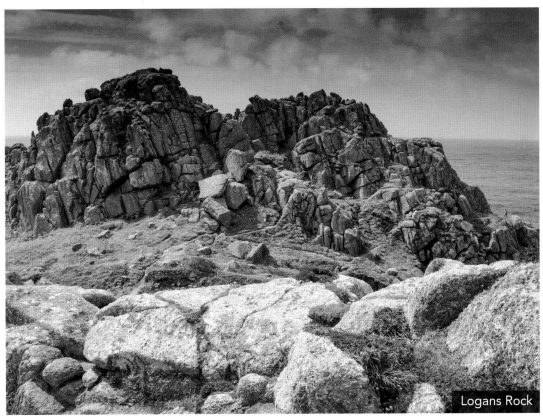

Logans Rock

Lizard Point showing disused Lifeboat station and Lighthouse complex on the summit

The Lizard
An Lysardh

The Lizard Peninsula in south-west Cornwall is within the Cornwall Area of Outstanding Natural Beauty and is recognised as being of international botanical importance - 15 of Britain's rarest plants can be found here as well as a colony of the rare 'Chough' crow. It is the most Southerly point of the British mainland.

The Owl (above) and the Pussycat (top left) rock formations with Lighthouse in the distance

Sea Campion

Bass Point lookout station

Thrift on the coastal path

Coastal cliffs on The Lizard

11

Mullion
Eglusvelyan

The civil parish of Mullion is the Lizard's largest village, with shops, restaurants, galleries, and a 15th century church in the village centre. Exhilarating coastal walks lead visitors along the cliffs, through Mullion Cove's beautiful working harbour and up onto Predannack Heath, while golden beaches welcome families and holidaymakers.

Looking down on Mullion Harbour

Boscastle
Kastel Boterel

The medieval fishing port of Boscastle lies along Cornwall's rugged north coast. Stone cottages and tea-rooms cluster round a picturesque natural harbour, where visitors can enjoy a leisurely walk and take in the majestic views. More challenging trails explore the cliffs above, before meandering inland and around verdant Valency Valley.

Early evening on Boscastle harbour

Boscastle tearoom. This was destroyed in the 2004 flood and was rebuilt to match the original structure.

The National Trust shop on the banks of the river

The Old Manor House pub

Padstow
Lannwedhenek

Situated on the River Camel estuary, Padstow is a lively town known for its stunning coastal scenery and delicious locally sourced food. Sandy beaches and charming coves offer boat rides, surfing and rock-pooling, while the famous Camel Cycle Trail provides access to some of North Cornwall's most beautiful countryside.

Padstow harbour

The harbour slipway

Harbour wall with the coastal village of Rock in the distance

Full view of the harbour

Port Isaac
Porthysek

A quaint fishing village home to sea-shanty singers, Port Isaac is composed of narrow streets and whitewashed cottages dating from the 18th and 19th centuries. In the summer, fishing and scenic trips run from the harbour, and superb walks along the coast or inland can be enjoyed all year round. It is also the location for the television series 'Doc Martin'.

Port Isaac harbour

Old anchor in the village

Main Street, Port Isaac

Stowaway Tea Shoppe

Looking down on the harbour

25

The Wayside Museum & Trewey Mill, Zennor village

The Gurnards Head pub, near Zennor

Zennor
Sen Senar

Zennor Village and church

The imposing cliffs at Zennor rise over 200 feet above the sea, giving fabulous views that D.H. Lawrence described as "infinite Atlantic, all peacock-mingled colours". From the Norman church, a circular walk leads sightseers through the ancient village and across wild, windswept moors to the spectacular summit of Zennor Hill.

Carn Galver Tin Mine ruin

Perranporth
Porthperan

Perranporth's miles of smooth sands and clear waters attract surfers and tourists year after year. The town offers golf courses, a boating lake and several historical sites. Explore the caves along the beach or embark on cliff walks to spot rare birds and a chorus of colourful wild flowers.

Main street, Perranporth

IN GRATEFUL MEMORY
OF THOSE WHO SERVED IN THE
1914 GREAT WAR 1918
FROM GRADE RUAN MAJOR & RUAN MINOR
AND ESPECIALLY OF THOSE WHO FELL
WHOSE NAMES ARE INSCRIBED BELOW
J.H. ARTHUR · W.T. CANNICOTT·E.C.HALL·
F.HALL   A.JANE   H.JANE·
W.LEGG·S.J.ROBINSON·W.T.STEVENS·
H.C.STONE·A.E.WAREHAM·E.W.WESCOMB·

1939 – ARTHUR G. BLOOMFIELD – 1945.

Ruan Minor village and church

Ruan Minor
Ruan Vyghan

The small village and former parish of Ruan Minor on the Lizard is home to thatched cottages, a traditional dairy farm and galleries selling local crafts. In 1934 the parish of Ruan Minor was united with the parishes of Ruan Major and Grade to form the new parish of Ruan-Grade.

Overgrown wall with deer stile

Gunnera at the roadside

Field path with Iris and footbridge

A TASTE OF THE CORNISH COASTLINE

ST. IVES • MEVAGISSEY • CRANTOCK • MOUSEHOLE